Jes
Nazareth
Who is He?

Jesus of Nazareth

Who is He?
Arthur Wallis

CHRISTIAN • LITERATURE • CRUSADE
Fort Washington, Pennsylvania 19034

CHRISTIAN LITERATURE CRUSADE
U.S.A.
P.O. Box 1449, Fort Washington, PA 19034

GREAT BRITAIN
51 The Dean, Alresford, Hants. SO24 9BJ

AUSTRALIA
P.O. Box 419M, Manunda, QLD 4879

NEW ZEALAND
10 MacArthur Street, Feilding

ISBN 0-87508-558-X

First North American edition 1962
This printing 2000

Printed in the United States of America

For the purposes of this inquiry the Author has followed the custom in most English Bibles of not using capitals for the personal pronouns referring to the Deity. Quotations are from the English Revised Version (unless otherwise stated) with Jehovah substituted for LORD (Hebrew: Yah or Yahwe) and Spirit for Ghost. Matter in brackets is the Author's.

Jesus OF NAZARETH
Who Is He?

*T*HE HISTORICAL existence of "Jesus of Nazareth" at the commencement of the Christian era is beyond dispute; it is witnessed to by those who did not believe in him as well as by those who did. What view are we to take of this historical personage and the remarkable claims that he made? In the first analysis the possibilities are confined to three: either he was a deceiver who made claims for himself knowing them to be untrue; or he was self-deceived, sincere but deluded, a man suffering from some kind of hallucination; or he was a man whose words and claims were sober truth. Some of the Jews of his day said that he was a deceiver. Would you agree that this describes the character of the author of the Sermon on the Mount? Do you think that the influence he has exerted on the world has been that of a deceiver? Others accused him of being deluded, out of his mind, "mad." Do you think that the influence of Jesus on the world has been that of a man mentally deranged? Would such a man be able so to speak that "the multitudes were astonished at his teaching," so to answer his critics that they were reduced to silence and dared not ask him any more

questions, and to compel his enemies to acknowledge, "Never man so spake"? If then we rule out
these two possibilities, we are left with the third,
and find ourselves forced to conclude that he was a
true man, who spoke the sober truth—a fact which
is borne out by the influence he has exerted upon
mankind.

The New Testament provides the only original
account in existence of Christ and his teaching. It is
not our present purpose to inquire into the claims of
the Bible to be the Word of God—that has been
fully and ably done by many others—but accepting
its veracity, to discover its teaching concerning Jesus
of Nazareth. Acknowledging that his claims and the
claims that Scripture makes for him are true, how
are we to understand them? Did he really claim to
be God manifest in the flesh, as Christendom has
generally maintained? Or might it not be more in
keeping with the facts to take the view that he was
the special sent one by God, but not God himself?
Was he the divine *uncreated* second person of an
eternal Godhead, or was he the supreme *created* being,
not equal with but inferior to God, though occupying
an exalted position with him?

"Does it matter very much?" some may ask. "Have
we time to bother with theological quibbles, or split-
ting hairs over fine points of doctrine?" Our answer
is that it is a question of vital import. If Jesus Christ
is God, then we must give him the worship due to
God; to deny it to him is to insult the Godhead. If
Jesus Christ is not God, then to worship him as

though he were, no matter how elevated or superior he may be as a created being, would be both blasphemy and idolatry. If Jesus Christ is God he is an infinite being, and between him and the highest creature is a gulf of infinite dimensions. If Jesus Christ is not God, then no matter how exalted a creature we may conceive him to be, there is between him and the one Jehovah the same infinite gulf.

Look at it this way: the mountaineer on the summit of Everest may be thought to be very far above the scientist in his bathysphere exploring the deepest ocean bed, but in fact the distance between them is infinitesimal when one considers how far both are from yonder star, millions of light-years distant from the earth. The mountain peak and the ocean bed belong to the sphere of earth, and their different elevations may be measured and compared; the star belongs to the sphere of the heavens, and therefore no intelligent comparison with earthly things is possible. I apply this to the question before us: Are we to think of Jesus Christ in terms of the star or the mountain peak? This impassable gulf that divides deity from mere humanity, the Creator from the creature, the infinite from the finite—does it separate him from God, or him from man?

THE PROBLEM

An inquiry such as this is plainly called for when we find that people who assert their faith in the truth of the Bible as God's word to man are funda-

mentally disagreed on how it is to be understood in
relation to its central figure, Jesus of Nazareth. It is
clear that Jesus claimed to be *the Son of God,* and
that the New Testament Scriptures endorse that
claim. But what does the expression mean? With
some it is synonymous with a claim to be God the
Son, to belong to the Godhead, to be equal with the
Father, and that it affirms unquestionably his deity.
Others are emphatic that it is not so; they point out
that angels are also sons of God,[1] but they are not
divine; believers may be called sons of God,[2] but
they have no claim to deity. Some will refer us to
that extraordinary assertion of Jesus, "I and the Father are one";[3] "What is this," they would say, "if
not a claim to equality with God?" Others will reply
that he was only asserting his harmony with the Father, and will quote in support John 17:21, and remind us also of his words, "the Father is greater than
I."[4] Some say that he claimed to be eternal and
uncreated when he said, "Before Abraham was, I
am."[5] Others assure us that he is but the first of
God's created beings, for does he not describe himself as "the beginning of the creation of God"?[6]

Clearly these two views are mutually exclusive;
they cannot both be right. There cannot be degrees
of deity; either Jesus Christ was God or he was not
God. Since both parties cite the Bible for their support, how are we to decide which is correct? The
fact that views can exist so diametrically opposed
may serve to teach us the fallibility of the unaided

---

[1] Job 1:6. [2] Romans 8:14. [3] John 10:30.
[4] John 14:28. [5] John 8:58. [6] Revelation 3:14.

human mind in the interpreting of the divine revelation, and to remind us of our utter dependence upon the divine Author of the book to be its Interpreter. As we appeal "to the law and to the testimony" for an answer to this question—and we can turn to no other authority—let us bear in mind three important principles. The first, that a sincere and open mind which is willing to be convinced by the truth is essential; as Jesus himself said, "If any man willeth to do [God's] will, he shall know of the teaching, whether it be of God."[1] The second, that for right interpretation a passage must be considered strictly in the light of its context, and in the light of other Scripture passages dealing with the same theme; ignoring this, we can make the Bible teach what we please. Finally, that we approach our inquiry with a humble prayer to Jehovah for his illumination: "Guide me in thy truth, and teach me; for thou art the God of my salvation."[2]

THE OLD TESTAMENT

The New is in the Old concealed;
The Old is in the New revealed. (Augustine)

The reading of the Old Testament is designed to prepare us for the New. What we find in full bloom in the New is but a seed in the Old. The seed may be small, it may be hidden, it may be shrouded in mystery—but it is there. This is particularly true concerning Jesus of Nazareth. It was during that

---

[1] John 7:17.   [2] Psalm 25:5.

memorable walk to Emmaus that "beginning from Moses and from all the prophets, he [Jesus] interpreted to them in all the [O.T.] scriptures the things concerning himself."[1] As we set out to discover who he really is, we must expect the Old Testament to point us down the road that leads to the truth, and prepare our minds for the fuller revelation to follow.

Every Jew knew from the sacred Hebrew Scriptures that man was not permitted to look upon God. "Thou canst not see my face: for man shall not see me and live."[2] The New Testament teaching is to the same effect: "No man hath seen God at any time,"[3] "dwelling in light unapproachable; whom no man hath seen, nor can see."[4] In view of this it is necessary to inquire who was the one who appeared to Abram as "the God of glory"?[5] To Hagar in the wilderness as "the angel of Jehovah," who testified, "Thou art a God that seeth. . . . Have I even here seen him who saw me"?[6] To Jacob at Peniel who said "I have seen God face to face, and my life is preserved"?[7] To Moses at the burning bush as "I am" so that he "hid his face; for he was afraid to look upon God"?[8] To Joshua near Jericho as "captain of the host of Jehovah" so that he "fell on his face to the earth, and did worship"?[9] To Gideon under the oak in Ophrah, who is described both as "the angel of Jehovah" and as "Jehovah"?[10] To Manoah and his wife, parents of Samson, who "fell on their faces to the ground. . . . And Manoah said unto his wife, We shall surely die, because we have seen God"?[11]

[1] Luke 24:27. [2] Exodus 33:20. [3] John 1:18.
[4] 1 Timothy 6:16. [5] Acts 7:2. [6] Genesis 16:13.
[7] Genesis 32:30. [8] Exodus 3:6. [9] Joshua 5:14.
[10] Judges 6:11–14. [11] Judges 13:20–22.

These incidents of Old Testament history must evoke important questions in the minds of thinking people. It is clear that these godly people were overwhelmed with fear because they were convinced that they had seen God.

They testified to their conviction, and Scripture endorses but does not explain their testimony. Some believed that they would die, and were surprised that they lived. Their relief when they were spared did not remove their conviction that they had seen God, nor did it remove their perplexity as to how it was they could see Him and live. If they did not truly see God, why does Scripture imply that they did? If they did see God, why did they not die according to Exodus 33:20? Why is the one who appeared to Gideon described one moment as the angel of Jehovah and the next as Jehovah himself? Similarly, why do we find the aged patriarch Jacob equating God with the angel that redeemed him when he blessed the sons of Joseph: "The God before whom my fathers Abraham and Isaac did walk, the God which hath fed me all my life long unto this day, the angel which hath redeemed me from all evil, bless the lads"?[1] Why did this angel command Moses and Joshua to take off their shoes from their feet? Why did he receive worship,[2] whereas, when the apostle John fell down before an angel to worship him he was told, "See thou do it not . . . worship God"?[3]

The person of Jesus who is the Christ provides the only solution to this enigma of the seeming ap-

---

[1] Genesis 48:15,16.   [2] Joshua 5:14.   [3] Revelation 19:10.

pearances of God in the Old Testament in the person of this mysterious angel of the covenant. He it was who, being "in the beginning with God,"[1] shared his glory before the universe existed.[2] If this angel of Jehovah (or angel of the covenant) was God's Son, then one thing is clear: the manifestation of the Son is presented in the Old Testament Scriptures as a manifestation of God, and explains why in the New Testament Jesus declared, "He that hath seen me hath seen the Father."[3] That this angel of Jehovah is also called Jehovah leads us to inquire whether the title Jehovah may not be applied to the Son as well as to the Father; this would account for the numerous passages in the Old Testament which speak of Jehovah but, when quoted in the New Testament, are related directly to Christ (see the appendix); this would also explain such a verse as Malachi 3:1, "The Lord, whom ye seek, shall suddenly come to his temple"—who could this be but Jehovah? But the prophet continues, "even the angel of the covenant, whom ye delight in." We thus conclude that though no mortal eye has gazed or can gaze on God the Father, yet in the person of his Son, who is the very image of his substance, men have truly seen God.

THE EXPRESSION OF GOD'S LOVE

The giving of the Son to redeem us is shown to be the expression of God's own love to mankind. "God so loved the world, that he gave his only be-

---

[1] John 1:2. [2] John 17:5. [3] John 14:9.

gotten Son."[1] "God commendeth his own love toward us, in that, while we were yet sinners, Christ died for us."[2] Such passages leave us with a deep impression of the immensity of God's love as expressed in him who is "his unspeakable gift."[3] Here is a love which passes knowledge—heights that we can never scale and depths that we can never plumb. Is it possible that this immeasurable gift was only the giving by God of a creature he had made? When God said to Abraham, "Take now thy son, thine only son, whom thou lovest, even Isaac . . . and offer him there for a burnt offering,"[4] he was giving us a foreshadowing of an infinitely greater sacrifice that he himself would make in a coming day.

God was not asking Abraham merely to yield up something he possessed or something he had made— an insignificant sacrifice by comparison—but his only son whom he had begotten, whom he dearly loved, who was part of himself. God was asking of him the greatest sacrifice possible in view of the promise, "In Isaac shall thy seed be called";[5] and by his unquestioning obedience and implicit faith Abraham commended his own love to God. In "offering up his only begotten son"[6] Abraham had offered up himself—he could give no more. But if Jesus was merely a created being, not sharing his Father's deity as Isaac shared his father's humanity, then there is no ground of comparison between the two; indeed, we ought to have far more admiration for the sacrifice of Abra-

---

[1] John 3:16.   [2] Romans 5:8.   [3] 2 Corinthians 9:15.
[4] Genesis 22:2.   [5] Hebrews 11:18.   [6] Hebrews 11:17.

ham on Moriah than that of God on Golgotha, for Abraham was giving himself but God was only giving a creature he had made. How could this be God commending "his own love"? How could it be true that on the cross God was giving himself, that he "was in Christ reconciling the world unto himself"?[1] If God could create one perfect son, and then give him for man's redemption, could he not in his omnipotence create a thousand others to replace him? How could this be "his great love wherewith he loved us,"[2] of which the responding love of man, even that of Abraham, is but a feeble, pale reflection?

THE WORD WAS

Only the eternal God is outside of time. All created beings belong to time since they have a beginning. The moment God put forth his power to create, time began. It is this commencement of time that is expressed by the phrase "In the beginning was the Word."[3] The context shows that it is God's Son who is "the Word." Just as a person's mind remains unknown and unknowable except as he gives utterance to his thoughts, so the eternal, invisible God is only known through the Son who is his utterance or Word. The verse tells us, "In the beginning the Word was." It does not say, "In the beginning the Word came to be," or "In the beginning the Word was created." Nothing could be simpler than the use of such expressions if they conveyed

---

[1] 2 Corinthians 5:19.   [2] Ephesians 2:4.   [3] John 1:1.

the truth. Since Genesis opens with the statement "In the beginning God created the heavens and the earth," why could not John's Gospel open with the statement "In the beginning God created the Word"? Why does it state instead that "In the beginning the Word was"? Why does it declare that when time began, the Word was already in existence? There can be only one answer: that he existed eternally.

It is significant that the Son is not called *a* Word, but *the* Word; Scripture gives no other means of the Father's expression but the Son. He, and he alone, is "the effulgence of his glory, and the very image of his substance."[1] The expression of God's mind in the creating of the world,[2] the upholding of the world,[3] the redeeming of the world,[4] has been effected through the activity of "the Word." As far as we can tell from Scripture, God has never expressed himself apart from the Word. Can we then conceive of a time when the Word was not, when the eternal God was without utterance or expression? Are we to believe that he was obliged to create the Word to express himself? Such a thought is surely incredible. The statement with which Scripture opens, "In the beginning God," finds its counterpart in the opening of John's Gospel, "In the beginning the Word," and prepares us to accept the tremendous statement that follows—to accept it without tampering with it to make it fit a theory—"the Word was God."[5]

---

[1] Hebrews 1:3.
[2] John 1:3.
[3] Hebrews 1:3.
[4] Colossians 1:14.
[5] John 1:1.

THE FATHER AND THE SON

In the cross-examination of a witness it is often the facts which emerge accidentally that provide the most convincing witness to the truth, just because they *are* unintentional rather than calculated and prepared. So it is with this theme in Scripture. Not only in the great doctrinal passages—so often the battleground of controversy—but in the most casual allusions and seemingly incidental statements scattered throughout Scripture, do we find pointers to the truth. For example, there are passages in which the name of the Son is linked with that of the Father in such a way, and in such connections, as to leave an honest inquirer in no doubt as to how the person of the Son is to be viewed. Let us look at some of them.

Jesus said, "If a man love me, he will keep my word: and my Father will love him, and *we* will come unto him, and make *our* abode with him."[1] And again, "But now have they both seen and hated *both me and my Father*."[2] Then in the epistles we read, "Grace to you and peace from God our Father and the Lord Jesus Christ."[3] "Now may our God and Father himself, and our Lord Jesus, direct our way unto you."[4] "Looking for the blessed hope and appearing of the glory of our great God and Saviour Jesus Christ."[5] Finally in the book of Revelation: "Salvation unto our God which sitteth on the throne, and unto the Lamb."[6]

---

[1] John 14:23.
[2] John 15:24.
[3] Romans 1:7.
[4] 1 Thessalonians 3:11.
[5] Titus 2:13.
[6] Revelation 7:10.

These are but a sample of the many that could be quoted. Do they not leave the reader with the strong impression that these persons belong to the same plane, the same order of being? When we find created beings innumerable, out of every nation under heaven, rendering to the Lamb the same ascription of worship and homage that they ascribe to the eternal God, how can we possibly think that this great gulf that separates the creature from the Creator separates him from *God* and not him from *man*? How would it sound to us if Scripture was to read, "Grace to you and peace from God our Father and Michael his archangel"? Or if Scripture led us to ascribe "Salvation unto our God which sitteth on the throne, and unto the angel Gabriel"? Then consider him who is seen in the above scriptures in company with the Father, indwelling those who believe and obey him, and who is, with the Father, the joint source of grace and peace to believing men, the joint director of the steps of his servants, the joint object of their ascriptions of worship. Is he merely a supreme spirit-creature? Is he only a kind of super-archangel who had a beginning in time, and might have an end if his Creator so desired?

CHRIST AND THE SPIRIT

"Who hath directed the Spirit of Jehovah?"[1] inquires the prophet. Plainly implied in the question is the answer, only Jehovah himself, as the rest of

---

[1] Isaiah 40:13.

the chapter emphasizes. No one but God could have authority to direct the Spirit of God. But if this is so, how do we account for the words of Jesus when he speaks of the Comforter, the Holy Spirit, as the one "whom *I* will send unto you from the Father,"[1] and again "If I go, *I* will send him unto you"?[2] It was also Jesus who breathed on the apostles in the upper room and said, in anticipation of Pentecost, "Take ye the Holy Spirit";[3] this act of breathing was perhaps symbolic, but it was also misleading and deceptive if Jesus had no authority to bestow the Spirit of God.

It is significant that Isaiah 40:13 may also be rendered, "Who hath *meted out* the Spirit of Jehovah?" (R.V. margin). Christ has done so, according to Peter on the day of Pentecost, for "being therefore by the right hand of God exalted, and having received of the Father the promise of the Holy Spirit, he [Jesus] hath poured forth [or meted out] this, which ye see and hear."[4] To Peter this was simply the fulfillment of the promise he had heard himself from Jesus: "I will send him unto you." Similarly had John the Baptist, the greatest of the prophets, borne witness to Jesus as the Bestower of the Spirit: "There cometh he that is mightier than I, the latchet of whose shoes I am not worthy to unloose: *he* shall baptize you with the Holy Spirit and with fire."[5] But if only God can direct the Spirit of God, and yet Scripture so clearly speaks of Christ directing the Spirit of God, how can we resist the conclusion that Christ is God?

---

[1] John 15:26. [2] John 16:7. [3] John 20:22.
[4] Acts 2:33. [5] Luke 3:16.

In further confirmation of this we find that the Spirit of God which inspired the prophets is described by Peter as "*the Spirit of Christ* which was in them";[1] and elsewhere the Spirit of God is described as "the Spirit of his Son,"[2] "the Spirit of Jesus Christ,"[3] "the Spirit of Jesus."[4] Since the New Testament reveals so conclusively that the special activity of the Spirit of God is toward Christ, that it is his peculiar task to "bear witness of Christ,[5] to glorify Christ,[6] to take of the things of Christ and declare them unto us,[7] how can he be less than God who not only bestows the divine Spirit but is the all-absorbing object of his activity?

CHRIST AND CREATION

Scripture has a characteristic expression for the whole universe, for all created things, animate or inanimate; it is the phrase "all things." "*All things* were made by him [the Son]."[8] "For in him were *all things* created . . . and he is before *all things*."[9] How could Christ exist before the "all things," the whole created universe, and create the "all things," while at the same time being part of them, which would be the case if he had been created by God? Notice how Scripture uses the timeless present that relates to the eternal existence of deity when it says, "he *is* [not was] before all [created] things."

---

[1] 1 Peter 1:11.
[2] Galatians 4:6.
[3] Philippians 1:19.
[4] Acts 16:7.
[5] John 15:26.
[6] John 16:14.
[7] John 16:15.
[8] John 1:3.
[9] Colossians 1:16,17.

We learn from the same passage in Colossians that the "all things" were created "in him," "through him," and "unto him." "Through him" suggests that he was the agent of the Father in creation (cp. Hebrews 1:2), but lest we should think that this means that the Son was "an inferior workman, creating simply for the glory of a higher Master, for a God superior to himself," it states: "all things have been created through him *and unto him*," that is, for his possession, his pleasure, and his glory. God is surely the end of all created beings, as the apostle affirms: " Of him, and through him, and unto him, are all things,"[1] but here in Colossians we see that Christ is the end of all created things, that they have been created "unto him." How then can we escape the conclusion that Christ is God?

The Bible teaches us that creation is a work peculiar to God, in which his character and glory are revealed to men. "I am Jehovah, and there is none else; beside me there is no God. . . . I form the light, and create darkness; I make peace and create evil [i.e., adversity]; I am Jehovah, that doeth all these things."[2] "For the invisible things of [God] since the creation of the world are clearly seen, being perceived through the things that are made, even his everlasting power and divinity; that they may be without excuse."[3] "Fear God, and give him glory; . . . and worship him that made the heaven and the earth and sea and fountains of waters."[4] If Jehovah created the world through an inferior being, who was him-

---

[1] Romans 11:36.   [2] Isaiah 45:5,7.   [3] Romans 1:20.
[4] Revelation 14:7.

self created, how can creation be that divine work which peculiarly sets forth Jehovah as the only God, the only one to be worshipped and adored, and which reveals uniquely his everlasting power and divinity, as these verses teach? If indeed Christ be a creature, by bestowing upon him such wisdom and power necessary to create all things, has not God subjected mankind to the grievous temptation of worshipping as God him through whom all things were created? If Jesus Christ be not God, then this very work of creation, designed to lead men to the knowledge of the true God, must of necessity invite them to worship and serve the creature, Christ, rather than the Creator, God.[1]

CHRIST THE REDEEMER

Throughout the Old Testament we discover that it is peculiarly and solely the work of Jehovah to be the Saviour and Redeemer of his people. How characteristic are such statements as these: "Beside me there is no Saviour";[2] "Salvation belongeth unto Jehovah";[3] "I Jehovah am thy Saviour, and thy Redeemer, the Mighty One of Jacob."[4] Heathen nations on the other hand are reproached for their folly in praying to gods that cannot save.[5] But in the New Testament the work of salvation and redemption is attributed to Christ, who came expressly to save his people from their sins, and who is twice designated as "the Saviour of the world."[6] If then,

---

[1] Romans 1:25. [2] Isaiah 43:11. [3] Psalm 3:8.
[4] Isaiah 49:26. [5] Isaiah 44:17; 45:20. [6] John 4:42; 1 John 4:14.

there is no Saviour but God, and Jesus is "the Saviour of the world," it is impossible to resist the conclusion that Jesus is God; the Jehovah Saviour of the Old Testament is the Saviour Christ of the New. This is confirmed by Isaiah 44:6 which reads: "Thus saith Jehovah, the King of Israel, and *his Redeemer Jehovah of Hosts: I am the first, and I am the last,*" for this description of Jehovah the Redeemer, "the first and the last," is three times attributed to Christ in the book of Revelation.[1]

Job's wonderful prophecy concerning the Redeemer is conclusive: "I know that my Redeemer liveth, and that he shall stand up at the last upon the earth: and after my skin hath been thus destroyed, yet from my flesh shall I see God: whom I shall see for myself, and mine eyes shall behold, and not another."[2] Two vital facts emerge from this wonderful statement: the one whom Job describes as "my Redeemer" must refer to Jesus Christ, since he is to stand up at the last upon the earth, and Job is to see him with his own eyes in the flesh; and secondly, this Redeemer is God.

CHRIST THE JUDGE

"Shall not the Judge of all the earth do right?"[3] Most men, however feeble their conception of God, have an innate conviction that there is a God of justice superintending the affairs of men. But when we learn that "God shall bring every work into judgment, with every hidden thing, whether it be good

---

[1] Revelation 1:17; 2:8; 22:13.   [2] Job 19:25–27.   [3] Genesis 18:25.

or whether it be evil,"[1] we are staggered at the immensity of the task. "Jehovah is a God of knowledge, and by him actions are weighed."[2] There is no rough and ready calculation in the court of heaven, for the divine judge weighs every act and metes out perfect justice. Every factor—mental, moral, and physical—must be taken into consideration; every action must be viewed in the light of heredity and environment, light and understanding, good and evil influence, motive and opportunity, deterrents and consequences. Who but an omniscient God, all-wise and all-knowing, is competent to judge accurately one life, or even one act of one life?

But we learn that the Father has renounced all responsibility in the matter of judgment and caused it all to devolve upon the Son, "for neither doth the Father judge any man, but he hath given all judgment unto the Son";[3] he, and he alone, shall "judge the alive and the dead,"[4] "judge the secrets of men,"[5] and "give unto each one of you according to your works."[6] Consider the myriads of moral beings, both heavenly and human, that shall be brought before him. Remember that in his hands will rest the decision concerning their eternal destiny. Reflect on the statement that "he hath given *all* judgment unto the Son." There will be no complex cases that he will find himself incompetent to handle, or reserve for a higher authority. Ponder the spectacle of that supreme court of the universe over which he will preside, and remember that the eternal destiny of those

---

[1] Ecclesiastes 12:14   [2] 1 Samuel 2:3.   [3] John 5:22.
[4] 2 Timothy 4:1.   [5] Romans 2:16.   [6] Revelation 2:23.

innumerable beings, their endless bliss or endless woe, will rest in his hands. No appeal will be possible; his decisions will be final, irrevocable, and eternal. From the face of the Son of Man seated upon his august throne they "shall go away into eternal punishment: but the righteous into eternal life."[1] If we believe the Scripture that the man Christ Jesus is to perform such an office, that man must be God.

THE CHARACTER OF CHRIST

That Scripture declares with one voice the absolute perfection of Christ's character cannot be gainsaid. Were it otherwise he could never have been the outshining of God's glory, and the very image of his substance. As we contemplate this one who is "holy, guileless, undefiled, separated from sinners,"[2] who is "without blemish and without spot,"[3] "who did no sin,"[4] "who knew no sin,"[5] and "in [whom] is no sin,"[6] let us ask ourselves what moral and spiritual perfections are attributed to Jehovah that are not also attributed to Christ?

Behold him who quietly affirmed, "I am the light of the world";[7] it was he, who, with one trenchant question, and one penetrating glance, caused his adversaries to slink away convicted by their own consciences,[8] or rendered them speechless with the unanswerable challenge "Which of you convicteth me of sin?"[9] It was he who wrung from the lips of a

---

[1] Matthew 25:46   [2] Hebrews 7:26.   [3] 1 Peter 1:19.
[4] 1 Peter 2:22.   [5] 2 Corinthians 5:21.   [6] 1 John 3:5.
[7] John 8:12.   [8] John 8:7–9.   [9] John 8:46.

reluctant Pilate the admission "I find no fault in this man,"[1] and moved a heathen centurion to exclaim in astonishment, "Certainly this was a righteous man."[2] It was he, who, in the depth of his agony, could so convince the criminal dying by his side that he declared, "This man hath done nothing out of place."[3] Does the Old Testament introduce us to Jehovah as the Holy One?[4] Then with equal emphasis is Jesus so called in the New.[5] How then can Jesus be one with Jehovah in moral and spiritual perfection, as Scripture presents him, if at the same time he is separated from him by that infinite gulf that parts deity from every other being? Furthermore, if Jehovah could create a sinless Christ, how was it that he ever saw fit to create Adam who could and did so quickly fall? Why did he not start the race with the sinless "last Adam" instead of the sinful first Adam?

The conversation of Jesus with the rich young ruler is significant. "Good teacher, what shall I do to inherit eternal life?" was the young man's question. "And Jesus said unto him, Why callest thou me good? none is good, save one, even God."[6] Let it be noted that Jesus did not deny that he was good, nor forbid his eager questioner calling him good; he merely asked him why he so addressed him. In the wording of the young ruler's question there was a latent contradiction, which Jesus was pointing out. The force of the Lord's question might be expressed thus: "You address me by the human title 'teacher' [cp. Luke 3: 12]

---

[1] Luke 23:4.   [2] Luke 23:47.   [3] Luke 23:41.
[4] Isaiah 40:25.   [5] Acts 3:14.   [6] Luke 18:18,19.

and yet you call me good; only God is good, and if I am acknowledged as truly good, then I must be acknowledged as truly God." Scripture not only sets forth the absolute goodness of Jesus Christ, but shows that absolute goodness and absolute deity are inseparable. It must be plainly understood that the denial of Christ's deity involves, on the authority of his own words quoted here, the denial of his essential goodness; the two stand or fall together.

THE CLAIMS OF CHRIST

In the fourth Gospel there are recorded three distinct instances of Jesus claiming to be the Son of God, and also, what is of the deepest significance, how that claim was understood. "For this cause therefore the Jews sought the more to kill him, because he not only brake the sabbath but also called God his own Father, making himself equal with God."[1] "The Jews answered him, For a good work we stone thee not, but for blasphemy; and because that thou, being a man, makest thyself God."[2] "The Jews answered [Pilate], We have a law, and by that law he ought to die, because he made himself the Son of God."[3]

These quotations establish two points beyond doubt. The first, that the Jews took for granted that the special claim of Jesus to be the Son of God and his calling "God his own Father" was nothing less than claiming divine equality with God, or making

---

[1] John 5:18.   [2] John 10:33.   [3] John 19:7.

himself God. Notice that Jesus never made any attempt to deny their assertion, or to show them that they had put the wrong construction on his claim. The second, that this claim of divine sonship, which the Jews plainly understood as a claim to deity, was the real issue in the trial before the Sanhedrin which issued in his crucifixion. A celebrated Jew, M. Salvador, has made it clear in his book *Jésus Christ,* that in view of the claims of Jesus, a Jew had no logical alternative to belief in his Godhood except the imperative duty of putting him to death. It is inconceivable that the Jews condemned him simply because they misunderstood the true nature of his claims. It is plain from the records that they put him to death because they saw clearly, yet refused to accept, the claims he was making. Of this Peter reminded them soon after, "Ye *denied* the Holy and Righteous One."[1]

Closely connected with his claim to be God's Son was his claim to be the Christ or the Messiah. What kind of Messiah had the Jewish prophets led their people to expect? Isaiah had described the coming one as "Emmanuel"—God with us,[2] as "the mighty God, the Father of eternity";[3] Jeremiah called him "Jehovah our righteousness";[4] Micah spoke of his eternal pre-existence;[5] Daniel predicted his everlasting dominion;[6] through Zechariah God refers to him as "the man that is my fellow";[7] while in Malachi his advent is described as the Lord coming suddenly

---

[1] Acts 3:14.
[2] Isaiah 7:14.
[3] Isaiah 9:6.
[4] Jeremiah 23:5,6.
[5] Micah 5:2.
[6] Daniel 7:14.
[7] Zechariah 13:7.

to his temple.[1] That the Jews looked upon his claim to be the Son of God as a claim to deity we have already seen. Clearly they linked with this his claim to be the Messiah, as we see from the solemn adjuration of the High Priest, "I adjure thee by the living God, that thou tell us whether thou be the Christ [or Messiah], the Son of God." From the Jewish standpoint the fate of Jesus was determined by his unhesitating reply, "Thou hast said [the truth]."[2]

CHRIST AND MANKIND

We have been seeking to discover from Scripture whether this impassable gulf that divides the Infinite from the finite, the Uncreated from the created, is a gulf that separates Christ together with all created beings, from God; or whether it separates Christ and God from them. The Scriptures considered thus far have shown beyond question that no such gulf ever existed between him and his Father, but that he possessed an identity of nature as "the only begotten Son." Therefore this impassable gulf must lie between him and all created beings. Does Scripture bear this out? Does it show man standing in the same relation to Christ as to God? Does it require that man shall render the same homage (that due from the creature to the Creator) to the Son as to the Father? One sentence will suffice to answer, perhaps the most conclusive on the subject to be found in Scripture, because it is virtually impossible

---

[1] Malachi 3:1.   [2] Matthew 26:63,64.

to make it mean anything other than what it says. From the lips of Jesus himself we learn that it is the express desire of the Father "that all may honor the Son, even as they honor the Father. He that honoreth not the Son honoreth not the Father which sent him."[1]

A zealous religious worker who denied the deity of Christ said to a Christian friend of the writer, "The difference between us is this: you make much of Christ, but we make much of Jehovah." Had the speaker understood the import of this verse he would have seen that the honor he refused to give to the Son he was thereby denying to the Father. The apostle Peter would say to such a one what he said to the deeply religious people of his day, "Ye denied the Holy and Righteous One"—though no doubt he would be ready to add, "I know that in ignorance ye did it, as did also your rulers."[2] That the honor due to the Father is due to the Son does not however hinge upon one proof text, but is the very warp and woof of the New Testament revelation concerning Christ. This may be established along four lines: knowing Christ; trusting Christ; praying to Christ; worshipping Christ.

KNOWING CHRIST

Spiritual life, eternal life, depends upon spiritual knowledge; not knowledge of Scriptural facts, not knowledge of a system of doctrine, but heart knowl-

---

[1] John 5:23.   [2] Acts 3:14,17.

edge of the only true God.[1] The vengeance of God will yet fall upon those who know him not.[2] But Scripture places the knowledge of the Son on the same level as the knowledge of the Father, and equally essential to the possession of eternal life: "And this is life eternal, that they should know thee the only true God, and him whom thou didst send, even Jesus Christ."[3] "If ye had known me, ye would have known my Father also."[4] Furthermore, knowing the Father depends upon the will of the Son to reveal him, for "neither doth any know the Father, save the Son, and he to whomsoever the Son willeth to reveal him";[5] hence the bestowing of eternal life upon men is in the hands of the Son.[6]

Paul shows us that his most intense desires and longings are for a fuller knowledge of Christ: "What things were gain to me, these have I counted loss *for Christ*. Yea verily, and I count all things to be loss for the excellency of *the knowledge of Christ Jesus* my Lord: for whom I suffered the loss of all things, and do count them but dung, *that I may gain Christ . . . that I may know him*, and the power of his resurrection, and the fellowship of his sufferings."[7] It is characteristic of all the apostle's teaching to emphasize that not only salvation but full spiritual maturity is bound up with the knowledge of Christ: "till we all attain unto the unity of the faith, and of *the knowledge of the Son of God*, unto a full-grown man, unto the measure of *the stature of the fullness of Christ*."[8]

---

[1] Jeremiah 31:34.   [2] 2 Thessalonians 1:8.   [3] John 17:3.
[4] John 14:7; cp. 2 Peter 1:2.   [5] Matthew 11:27.   [6] John 10:28; 17:2.
[7] Philippians 3:7–10.   [8] Ephesians 4:12,13.

Since the knowledge of the Son is the key to the knowledge of the Father, and since there is at least as much emphasis placed upon the knowledge of the one as the other, how can we escape the conclusion that Christ is God?

TRUSTING CHRIST

The New Testament does not present salvation as being available in the name of Jehovah, but in the name of Jesus Christ of Nazareth, "for neither is there any other name under heaven, that is given among men, wherein we must be saved."[1] It is faith in Christ alone that justifies a man before God,[2] and saves him from his sin.[3] But this faith that saves is no intellectual assent to the truth of Christ's existence, or even the nature of his work. "Thou believest that God is One; thou doest well: the demons also believe, and shudder."[4] Such a faith does not deliver demons from their misery, nor does it save men from their sin. It must be "*with the heart* man believeth unto righteousness,"[5] and the heart includes not only the mind but also the affections and the will. The mind perceives him who is the object of faith; the affections embrace him; the will yields to him. The heart is thus captivated—mind, affections, and will— by the object of its faith. In a sense the believer merges his personal existence with the one in whom he believes; he is "joined" to Christ,[6] he is "in Christ"

---

[1] Acts 4:10–12.　　[2] Romans 3:22–26.　　[3] Acts 16:31.
[4] James 2:19.　　[5] Romans 10:10.　　[6] Romans 7:4; 1 Cor. 6:17.

(this and equivalent expressions are found about 100 times in Paul's writings), and can affirm "Christ liveth in me."[1]

If then Christ is truly the object of saving faith, as Scripture declares, and if this saving faith is of such a quality as to involve the voluntary submission of one's whole inner being—mind, affections, and will—to him, so that one is transplanted into a new spiritual sphere, "in Christ," and so transformed as to become "a new creature,"[2] can we really believe that this one who is to be thus trusted, depended upon, submitted to—who thus becomes the very sphere of our spiritual existence—is less than God? What measure of trust is the believer to give to the Almighty over and above what Scripture requires him to give to the Son of God?

PRAYING TO CHRIST

All prayer, as we properly understand the word, is only rightly addressed to God. In this, unitarians who deny Christ's deity and trinitarians who affirm it, are agreed. But according to the former, prayer should not be made to Christ, for he is not God; according to the latter, prayer may be made to Christ, for he is God. What saith the Scripture? Do we find any examples of praying to Christ? Are believers forbidden or encouraged to pray to him?

There are many in the gospel narratives who came and "besought" Jesus,[3] but can we be sure that this

---

[1] Galatians 2:20.   [2] 2 Corinthians 5:17.   [3] Matthew 14:36.

was praying to him as God? He said to the woman at the well, "If thou knewest the gift of God, and who it is that saith to thee, Give me to drink; thou wouldest have asked of him, and he would have given thee living water."[1] If we believe that that gift is available today, on the same conditions, how does praying to Christ to give us "living water" differ essentially from praying to God for his blessing? How does the prayer of David, "Have mercy upon me, O God,"[2] differ essentially from the cry of Bartimaeus, "Jesus, thou Son of David, have mercy on me"?[3] Similar words addressed to Christ have surely formed the saving prayer of multitudes who have passed from death to life. Certainly Paul's prayer to Christ, "Lord, what wilt thou have me to do?"[4] was the turning point in his experience of conversion. Are we then permitted to call on Christ at the first for salvation, but thereafter never to call on him again? Let Stephen, the first Christian martyr, answer it, when "full of the Holy Spirit," he finished his Christian course as Paul had commenced his, with a prayer to Christ: "Lord Jesus, receive my spirit."[5] Almost the same words that Jesus uttered to the Father at the cross, Stephen prayed to Christ at his martyrdom.

There is, in fact, abundant Scriptural evidence that praying to Christ was the rule, not the exception, among the early Christians, for they are characteristically described as those "calling on the name of Christ."[6] Then there are those breathings of the

---

[1] John 4:10.
[2] Psalm 51:1.
[3] Mark 10:47.
[4] Acts 9:6, A.V.
[5] Acts 7:55,59.
[6] Acts 9:14,20,21; 22:16; 1 Corinthians 1:2.

sacred writers, which are themselves prayers: "I hope in the Lord Jesus";[1] "I thank . . . Christ Jesus our Lord."[2] In fact, the last prayer of the Bible, expressing what has been the longing of the church down the years, is a prayer addressed to Christ: "Come, Lord Jesus." Isaiah rightly reminds us: "They have no knowledge that . . . pray unto a god that cannot save,"[3] but those who call upon Christ are praying unto one who is "able to save to the uttermost them that draw near unto God through him."[4] Those who have cried to him and received his gracious answer, cannot doubt that they have truly communed with God.

WORSHIPPING CHRIST

The worship of created beings is due to Jehovah and to him alone, for the Scripture says, "Thou shalt worship Jehovah thy God, and him only shalt thou serve."[5] To worship any other god, whether spirit-being, angel, or man-made image, is idolatry. If it can be shown from Scripture that men are enjoined not to worship Christ, and that he himself refused that worship which was due to God, then there is strong evidence that he was not truly divine. If on the other hand Scripture gives overwhelming evidence that men did worship him as God, and that he readily received it, and if we find that God encourages men to worship him, then the proof of his deity is conclusively established.

---

[1] Philippians 2:19.
[2] 1 Timothy 1:12.
[3] Isaiah 45:20.
[4] Hebrews 7:25.
[5] Matthew 4:9,10.

The word in the Greek Testament meaning to worship[1] occurs about sixty times, and is used generally to refer to that adoration which is due to God, but which men in their ignorance sometimes give to other men, or in their folly to gods, the work of their own hands. We find godly men refusing such worship from their fellows, as when Peter refused the worship of Cornelius,[2] or as when Paul and Barnabas in great consternation forbade the inhabitants of Lystra from doing sacrifice to them.[3] So it was with the angels: twice John, in the visions of Patmos, would have worshipped the angel that showed him such great revelations, and twice he was met with the same firm refusal, "See thou do it not . . . worship God."[4] But the worship angels refused to receive from men, "a multitude of the heavenly host" readily gave to the infant Jesus at his birth, and this at God's express command, "Let all the angels of God worship him."[5] What Jesus resolutely refused to do to Satan, the wise men did to the infant Son of God: "they fell down and worshipped him."[6] The worship of Jesus Christ by men is recorded throughout the gospel narratives: by the leper,[7] the ruler of the Jews,[8] the blind man,[9] the disciples in the boat,[10] the Canaanitish woman,[11] the mother of James and John,[12] the Gadarene demoniac;[13] in his resurrection, the two Marys;[14] at his ascension, the eleven disciples.[15]

---

[1] proskuneō.
[2] Acts 10:25,26.
[3] Acts 14:14,15.
[4] Revelation 19:10; 22:8,9.
[5] Hebrews 1:6.
[6] Matthew 2:11.
[7] Matthew 8:2
[8] Matthew 9:18.
[9] John 9:38.
[10] Matthew 14:33.
[11] Matthew 15:25.
[12] Matthew 20:20.
[13] Mark 5:6.
[14] Matthew 28:9.
[15] Matthew 28:17.

Are we to believe that this worship of Christ was merely the payment of reverence due to a great teacher, or of honor to a great benefactor, who under God had blessed them greatly in healing their bodies or saving their souls? Such a view is faced with insuperable difficulties. The man born blind gave no worship or homage to the one who had healed him until Jesus told him who he was; but when he knew that Jesus was the Son of God he worshipped him.[1] Clearly, then, he did not worship him for what he had done but for what he was. May we then take the view that this worship bestowed on Jesus, the Messiah, was something less than the worship due to Jehovah? The book of Revelation provides the conclusive answer, for it is the revelation of a person who is variously described as the First and the Last, the Alpha and the Omega, the King of kings and Lord of lords, the Lamb which is in the midst of the throne. Such was the opening vision of this glorious person that John records, "when I saw him, I fell at his feet as one dead."[2] He ascribes to him "the glory and the dominion for ever and ever."[3] He shows us myriads of angels round about the throne "saying with a great voice, Worthy is the Lamb . . . to receive the power, and riches, and wisdom, and might, and honor, and glory, and blessing."[4] Is this the sort of praise we would expect created spirits to render to a fellow created spirit, however exalted? Is this worship of an inferior quality to that which is rendered to the Almighty?

---

[1] John 9:35–38.　　[2] Revelation 1:17.　　[3] Revelation 1:5,6.
[4] Revelation 5:11, 12.

Notice how the vision continues: "And every created thing which is in the heaven, and on the earth, and under the earth, and on the sea, and all things that are in them, heard I saying, Unto him that sitteth on the throne, *and unto the Lamb,* be the blessing, and the honor, and the glory, and the dominion, for ever and ever."[1] Let it be noted that all created things in the universe are here ascribing homage to their Creator. Is the Lamb found among them ascribing homage to his Creator also? Or is he found receiving from all created beings precisely the same homage, the same ascription of worship that is addressed to the Almighty?[2] Earlier statements of Scripture should have prepared us for such scenes. Jesus had revealed that it was the Father's express desire "that all men should honor the Son, even as they honor the Father."[3] Paul reminds us that God has decreed "that in the name of Jesus every knee should bow, of [created] things in heaven and on earth and under the earth, and that every tongue should confess that Jesus Christ is Lord, to the glory of God the Father."[4] How clearly these verses teach that the glory of the Father is bound up forever in the glory of the Son.

Has not God said, "I am Jehovah; that is my name: and my glory will I not give to another"?[5] How then do we find him sharing his glory with the Lamb in the midst of the Throne? It can only be that he does not view his Son as "another" of an inferior order, but as "the man that is my fellow" or equal, and so

---

[1] Revelation 5:13.   [2] cp. Revelation 7:10.   [3] John 5:23.
[4] Philippians 2:10,11.   [5] Isaiah 42:8.

entitled to the honor and glory due to the Godhead. This is clearly how Paul interprets it, for at one place he exhorts, "He that glorieth, let him glory in the Lord,"[1] and at another he shows that it is one of the characteristics of saints that they "glory in Christ Jesus."[2]

Sir John Kennaway, Bart., of Escot, grandfather of the present Sir John, and a fine Christian gentleman, was once incorrectly addressed by a friend of the writer as "My Lord." Immediately he replied, "I am not entitled to that." This was the reaction of an upright and honest man, to refuse at once an honor to which he knew he was not entitled. But when Jesus was worshipped by Thomas with those remarkable words, "My Lord and my God,"[3] he not only received them, but gently rebuked Thomas for taking so long to believe the truth. And have you, my reader, ever worshipped him thus? Or are you among the multitudes, some religious and some otherwise, who honor not the Son, and therefore honor not the Father who hath sent him?[4]

CHRIST OUR RECONCILIATION

Whether or not Christ is worshipped is not the only matter affected by one's verdict concerning his deity. It vitally affects something even more basic, for the whole question of man's reconciliation to God hinges upon who Jesus is. The reader's personal salvation is at stake, for the Lord Jesus says today, as

---

[1] 1 Corinthians 1:31. [2] Philippians 3:3; 1:26. [3] John 20:28.
[4] John 5:23.

he said to religious people long ago, "Except ye believe that I am he, ye shall die in your sins."[1] Did not Jesus reveal that Peter's confession, "Thou art the Christ, the Son of the living God,"[2] is the very rock upon which the church is built?

Centuries before Jesus came, Job expressed his longing for a mediator, one who would arbitrate on his behalf with God. The Almighty seemed too exalted, too remote to contemplate dealing directly with him. "For he is not a man, as I am, that I should answer him, that we should come together in judgment. There is no daysman [umpire] betwixt us, that might lay his hand upon us both."[3] Job's longing for a daysman found fulfillment in the "one mediator between God and men, the man Christ Jesus."[4] He it is, and only he, who may lay his hand upon them both, for being "in the form of God" he was "made in the likeness of men,"[5] and so "the Word [which] was God . . . became flesh and dwelt among us."[6] To lay his hand upon God and man, as Job expressed it, required that he should be able to make personal contact with God in the divine realm and with man in the human realm. So it was that in the fullness of time Jesus came from "the bosom of the Father"[7] to be "born of a woman."[8] As to his knowledge of God, he confessed, "neither doth any know the Father, save the Son";[9] as to his knowledge of man, "he needed not that any one should bear witness concerning man; for he himself knew what was

---

[1] John 8:24.
[2] Matthew 16:16–18.
[3] Job 9:32.
[4] 1 Timothy 2:5, A.V.
[5] Philippians 2:6,7.
[6] John 1:1,14.
[7] John 1:18.
[8] Galatians 4:4.
[9] Matthew 11:27.

in man."[1] Only as the God-man could the Son be an effective mediator, representing God to man no less truly than man to God.

Some have asserted that only a man who was perfect, not divine, was required to ransom man from the power of sin, for the apostle states, "For as through the one man's disobedience the many were made sinners, even so through the obedience of the one [Jesus] shall the many be made righteous."[2] The view has been expressed thus in *Let God be True* (Watchtower Bible and Tract Society): "That which was lost [by Adam's transgression] was perfect human life, with its rights and earthly prospects. That which is redeemed or brought back [by Christ's sacrifice] is what was lost, namely, perfect human life, with its rights and earthly prospects. God's just law, at Deuteronomy 19:21, was that like should go for like, hence a perfect human life sacrificed for a perfect human life lost" (page 114). "Of all God's faithful creatures in heaven, it pleased him to use this One most dear to him, sending him to earth to become a perfect man, so carrying forward among other things the ransoming work" (page 115). "As a perfect man, Jesus stood in a position like that once occupied by the perfect Adam in the garden of Eden" (page 118).

That "a perfect human life" was necessary for the work of redemption is of course true, but where are we to find perfection outside of deity? This has already been made clear by our study of the character of Jesus, and his own words, "none is good, save one,

---

[1] John 2:25. [2] Romans 5:19.

that is God." A perfect human life is a spiritual and moral impossibility unless deity puts on humanity, and God becomes flesh. A perfect state is more than an innocent or even sinless state, as that of Adam before the fall, but a state that after being tested in its sinlessness has triumphed. So it was with Christ, "He suffered; and *having been made perfect* [through trial], he became unto all them that obey him the author of eternal salvation."[1] To speak of "the perfect man Adam in the garden" is to confuse innocence with perfection, and to misunderstand completely the nature of the perfection of Christ that qualified him to redeem. The statement that "like should go for like" refers to temporal punishment for sin,[2] and has no application to redemption in the case of Adam and Christ. Adam's sin was limited, though far-reaching in its effects; Christ's sacrifice is infinite in its embrace. From this very passage in Romans 5 it is clear that here is no question of "like for like," or "a perfect human life sacrificed for a perfect human life lost." See how it reads:

"But *not* as the trespass, so also is the free gift. For if by the trespass of the one the many died, *much more* did the grace of God, and the gift by the grace of the one man, Jesus Christ, *abound* unto the many. And *not* as through one that sinned, so is the gift: for the judgment came of one unto condemnation, but the free gift came of many trespasses unto justification. For if, by the trespass of the one, death reigned through the one; *much more* shall they that

---

[1] Hebrews 5:8,9. [2] Deuteronomy 19:21.

receive *the abundance of grace* and of the gift of righteousness reign in life through the one, even Jesus Christ."[1] Had Romans 5:19 been interpreted in the light of its context, the view under consideration would never have been expressed, for it is the negation of what the apostle is saying; he is not comparing but *contrasting* what was lost through Adam's transgression with what is bestowed through Christ's obedience. Notice how he describes what we may have in Christ: "much more," "the abundance of grace," "reigning in life." What did Adam know of these before he fell? Let the apostle sum up the argument in his own words (verse 20): "Where sin abounded, grace did abound more exceedingly." Here is warrant enough for the sentiments of the hymn:

> *In Christ the sons of Adam boast*
> *More blessings than their father lost.*

If, as some affirm, the sacrifice of Christ only avails to put the ransomed back where Adam was before he fell, then there is all the dire possibility that they shall again stumble as he did, and perish eternally. Is this then the "so great salvation" that Christ procured at such a price, which the apostle describes as "much more," "the abundance of grace," "reigning in life"? Surely no one who has tasted it would ever be tempted to think so.

Furthermore, if it were true that like must go for like, and that the sacrifice of the Redeemer must be at least equivalent in value to the being or beings he

---

[1] Romans 5:15–17.

is to redeem, then it is obvious that the sacrifice of one perfect but finite life (if such could exist) could only suffice to atone for the sin of one other finite life. On this basis Christ may be considered to have atoned for the sin of Adam, but not of his posterity. But Scripture teaches that Jesus is "the Saviour of the world";[1] he was sent "that the world should be saved through him";[2] "he is the propitiation for our sins; and not for ours only, but also for the whole world."[3] Further, it is clear that angelic beings and even the very heavens have been defiled,[4] and that the sacrifice of Christ avails to purge these also.[5]

Consider for a moment the cosmic nature of this redemption, that a sacrifice was needed which would embrace in its scope the millions upon millions of created beings, past, present, and future, and which would purge the heavens and reconcile them to God; is it conceivable that the shed blood of a sinless Adam could have accomplished it? Could a Michael or a Gabriel, though he were without blemish or without spot, take human form, become obedient unto death, and thus effect so great salvation? Here was a work not merely of saving souls from death, but of "bringing many sons unto glory,"[6] redeeming his people from all iniquity, and presenting "the church to himself a glorious church, not having spot or wrinkle or any such thing."[7] Let the wonder of it dawn upon the reader, and never again will he have

---

[1] John 4:42; 1 John 4:14.
[2] John 3:17.
[3] 1 John 2:2, (see also 1 Timothy 4:10; John 1:29; Titus 2:11; 2 Corinthians 5:19.)
[4] Job 4:18; 15:15; 25:5.
[5] Colossians 1:20; Hebrews 9:23.
[6] Hebrews 2:10.
[7] Ephesians 5:27.

doubts as to the nature of him who accomplished it. An infinite redemption requires an infinite Redeemer: "I Jehovah am thy Saviour, and thy Redeemer."[1]

Examination must now be made of some of the arguments used by those who deny that Christ is God.

THE BEGINNING OF THE CREATION OF GOD

Revelation 3:14 is sometimes cited as proof that Jesus Christ was created, and so is inferior to God. It reads: "To the angel of the Church in Laodicea write; These things saith the Amen, the faithful and true witness, *the beginning of the creation of God."* This last descriptive title is interpreted to mean that Jesus was the first being that God created. Let us put this to the test. This word "beginning"[2] is only found twice elsewhere in Revelation. In 21:6 God says "I am the Alpha and the Omega, the beginning and the end." No one who believes in God at all would suggest that this means that God had a beginning, or that he will one day have an end, but rather that he *is* the beginning and the end of everything, the originator and terminator of all that exists.

The other mention of this word is in 22:13 and is almost identical, "I am the Alpha and the Omega, the first and the last, the beginning and the end"; but this time the speaker is the one who says in the preceding verse, "Yea: I come quickly," and to whom his people respond in verse 20, "Amen: come, Lord

---

[1] Isaiah 49:26.   [2] Greek: archē.

Jesus." So the Son is also with the Father the originator and the terminator, the first cause, who will
bring to its consummation all that he has commenced.
How then can he himself be created? No, indeed;
the word "beginning" in Revelation 3:14 carries its
primary meaning of *origin*, as in these other two
instances of the word in the book of Revelation;
Christ Jesus is "the origin of the creation of God,"
the one who gave beginning to that creation, and to
this fact Scripture testifies with one voice.[1] He is
also "the firstborn of all creation," which emphasizes
his heirship, the one destined to inherit all that he
created, so the passage continues, "all things have
been created through him, and *unto him*."[2]

CHRIST HIGHLY EXALTED

To some, the statement "Wherefore also God
highly exalted him [Jesus]"[3] creates a difficulty. If
Christ were God then he already held the place of
absolute supremacy in the universe; how then could
he be exalted? We have only to examine the passage
in its context and the difficulty is resolved. The question may be answered by asking another, suggested
by the two preceding verses: How could one who
Scripture declares was "in the form of God," was
"with God," and "was God," empty himself and
humble himself?[4] The answer: By "taking the form
of a bondservant, being made in the likeness of men

---

[1] John 1:3; Colossians 1:16.
[2] Colossians 1:15,16; Hebrews 1:2.
[3] Philippians 2:9.
[4] Philippians 2:7,8.

. . . becoming obedient unto death." This involved the greatest act of self-humbling the universe has ever seen, or ever shall see; and it is this supreme example of divine humility that the apostle is holding up to the Philippian Christians. That "God highly exalted him" is but the complementary truth, and only what we should have expected. What should stagger us is not that he has been highly exalted, but that he who was "in the form of God" should ever have humbled himself for the salvation of sinful men. Is it not right and proper that we should now "behold the Son of Man ascending where he was before"?[1] It was for this that he had requested his Father when he said, "O Father, glorify thou me with thine own self with the glory which I had with thee before the world was."[2]

A number of years ago, after a meeting in the Chicago Tabernacle, a servant of God had conversation with a cultured young German, son of a rationalistic theologian. He found him to be a sincere seeker after the truth, but one who met grave difficulties in the New Testament, one of which was the seeming contradictions in Christ's own testimony concerning himself. "He says in one place, 'I and the Father are one'; and again, 'He that hath seen me hath seen the Father.' . . . But he says on another occasion that his Father was greater than he. Now he cannot be one with God and at the same time inferior to God. And he says, 'All authority hath been given unto me.' Now that is an admission that he had not power himself, but it was given to him;

---

[1] John 6:62.   [2] John 17:5.

and surely he that receives power is inferior to him that gives it. Now are not these contradictions in his own testimony?"

Having read aloud the passages mentioned, the Christian replied: "Suppose you had been on earth when Jesus was here and had heard him make these apparently contradictory statements, and had asked him. . . . And suppose he had said in reply, 'My child, what if, for the purpose of your redemption from sin and the curse of the law, I voluntarily laid aside my eternal glory, and suffered myself to be born of a woman, and made under the law, thus limiting my being to the condition of your nature, that I might, in that nature, offer up to God a sacrifice for sin that would enable him to proclaim forgiveness of sins to the whole world? In such a case, can you not conceive that there is no contradiction in these sayings of mine? For indeed I am one with the Father, and he that hath seen me hath seen the Father; but for the purposes of the atonement I have voluntarily assumed an inferior position, that I might take your place and die, which I could not have done unless I had taken a subordinate place, yea, and your very nature. Thus I sometimes speak of my eternal relation to God, and sometimes of my relation to him as the messenger of the covenant sent forth to redeem.'"

He listened attentively to this, and then said as if speaking to himself: "Yes, that might be; I can see how that might be. But did Christ ever make such an explanation? Is that the theory of Christ's subordination to the Father?"

Turning to Philippians chapter two the Christian replied: "Certainly this is the explanation of it; for see, Paul was trying to inculcate lessons of humility by exhorting the Philippians to take voluntarily a subordinate place in relation to each other, though they might as a matter of fact and right stand on an equality. He enforced his exhortation by this reference, 'Have this mind in you, which was also in Christ Jesus: who, being in the form of God, counted it not a prize [a treasure to be tightly grasped[1]] to be on an equality with God, but emptied himself, taking the form of a servant, being made in the likeness of men; and being found in fashion as a man, he humbled himself, becoming obedient even unto death, yea, the death of the cross.' "

The young man took the Bible in his hand, and read the passage over and over to himself, and said: "Wonderful! Wonderful!" And still holding the Book in his hand, with quivering chin and moistened eyes he said: "Yes, the Son of God made himself of no reputation *for me*, and took my nature and died on the cross *for me!*" And then looking up into the Christian's face, he said: "What have I got to do about it?"

"Accept him; believe on him; and confess him as your Saviour."

"May I?"

God's servant replied by opening his Bible to Romans 10:9: "If thou shalt confess with thy mouth Jesus as Lord, and shalt believe in thine heart that God raised him from the dead, thou shalt be saved."

"Let me see that!"

---

[1] Weymouth.

The book was handed to him, and he read it aloud, and then said: "I do believe in my heart that God raised him from the dead; and I do acknowledge him as my Saviour."

Together they dropped upon their knees while the servant of God gave thanks for his conversion, and committed him to God's keeping. (From *Taking Men Alive* by C. G. Trumbull.)

CHRIST'S INTERCESSION

The intercessory work of Christ on behalf of his people has been thought to imply an inferiority to God. How can he make supplication to God and yet be equal with God? Since this work of intercession is a direct result of his becoming man, the foregoing has already answered the difficulty. We have not found anything in Scripture to suggest that he thus interceded before he was made flesh; but having been found in fashion as a man, having suffered for sin, and risen again, he has entered "into heaven itself, now to appear before the face of God for us."[1] Scripture is emphatic that we are represented in heaven, not by "a glorious spirit-creature," but by a glorified man, the man Christ Jesus. Scripture states explicitly that it was "the Son of Man"[2] whom Stephen saw standing at God's right hand, and that it is "the Son of Man"[3] whom men shall yet see "coming on the clouds of heaven." Our present mediator *is* (not was) "the man Christ Jesus."[4] His intercession is part

---

[1] Hebrews 9:24. [2] Acts 7:56. [3] Matthew 26:64.
[4] 1 Timothy 2:5, A.V.

of his mediatorial work, and in direct consequence of his suffering as man. He could never intercede as our great high priest apart from his humanity. "For every high priest, *being taken from among men*, is appointed for men in things pertaining to God. . . . So Christ also. . . ."[1] Only as man is he touched "with the feeling of our infirmities."[2]

But it must be emphasized that it is by his very presence that Christ intercedes for his own. "He does not bend as a suppliant before the sanctity of God; he is a priest upon his throne.[3] Christ's perpetual presentation of himself before the Father is that which constitutes his intercession" (Liddon). "He ever liveth to make intercession" means that his very existence in the presence of God in all the worthiness of his person, and in all the sufficiency of his finished work, constitutes a perpetual plea on behalf of his people. His very appearing before the face of God is "for us."[4] We have seen the nature of his intercession, and have observed that it hinges upon his humanity, which in turn depends upon that gigantic step which exchanged "the form of God" for "the form of a bondservant"; instead of viewing all this as a reason for belittling his person and position, it should only serve to magnify the greatness of his grace. "For ye know the grace of our Lord Jesus Christ, that, though he was rich, yet for your sakes he became poor, that ye through his poverty might become rich."[5]

---

[1] Hebrews 5:1,5.   [2] Hebrews 4:15.   [3] Zechariah 6:13.
[4] Hebrews 9:24.   [5] 2 Corinthians 8:9.

THE SON SUBORDINATE TO THE FATHER

There are other verses of Scripture which some have thought imply that the Son is inferior to the Father. Christ said himself, "the Father is greater than I."[1] It is also said of Christ, "he shall deliver up the kingdom to God, even the Father . . . then shall the Son also himself be subjected to him that did subject all things unto him, that God may be all in all."[2] Can we give full weight to these important passages without contradicting what has been asserted concerning the deity of Christ? The answer is, undoubtedly yes.

Scripture helps us to understand the mystery of the divine order by pointing us to the human order: "the head of the woman is the man; and the head of Christ is God."[3] In other words, God is the head of Christ in the same way as the man is the head of the woman. Although in the human realm headship is invested in the man and not the woman, surely no one would think that the woman was thereby an inferior being to the man. The man is no more a human being than the woman because he is the head; the woman is no less a human being than the man because she is subordinate. The question of subordination does not touch the question of essential being. Just so in the realm of the Godhead. Here too there is equality of being, but a difference of order. Because the Son is and ever shall be subordinate to the Father, he is not one whit less God than the Father is. In his essential being the Son is equal to

---

[1] John 14:28.   [2] 1 Corinthians 15:24,28.   [3] 1 Corinthians 11:3.

the Father, but in respect to order within the Godhead he would say, "the Father is greater than I."

Scripture presents Christ as coming forth from God.[1] We might express it thus: the Father is the source of deity, the Son deity in its outflow; but as in the stream is all the fullness of the spring, so in Christ "dwelleth all the fullness of the Godhead bodily."[2] "God is a sun,"[3] but Christ is "the effulgence [or outshining] of his glory."[4] The full glory of the sun is concentrated in its rays. What would we know of the light and heat of the sun apart from its rays? Similarly, what would mankind have ever known of the glory of God apart from him who is the shining forth of that glory? Just as the sun's rays are part of the sun, so is Christ of the essence of the Godhead. As there could never have been a time when the sun existed without its rays, so could there never have been a time when God existed without Christ. They are coeternal. We could never say that the sun proceeds from its rays, but rather that the rays proceed from the sun; yet they are in essence one. Even so it would be erroneous to put Christ in the place of God the Father, for he comes forth from the Father, yet can he truly say, "I and the Father are one."[5]

ONE GOD

To some there may still be a grave difficulty in accepting the deity of Christ. How can the acknowl-

─────────────────────────────

[1] John 8:42; 13:3.   [2] Colossians 2:9.   [3] Psalm 84:11.
[4] Hebrews 1:3.   [5] John 10:30.

edging of another beside the Father within the Godhead be reconciled with the essential unity of God as taught in Scripture: "Jehovah our God is one Jehovah"?[1] This verse Jesus himself quoted, notwithstanding his own clear and unequivocal claim to deity. Evidently he saw nothing inconsistent or incompatible in the two truths; neither shall we when we rightly understand the nature of the unity of the Godhead.

Those who believe in the deity of Jesus Christ are not polytheistic; they believe in one God, one Jehovah, and that the unity of the Godhead is absolute, but they have not found anything in Scripture to suggest that Jehovah our God is *one person*. Such an assertion would be contrary to the whole Biblical revelation concerning the nature of the Godhead. Jesus said, "I and my Father are one," but not one person. When Scripture says "one Jehovah," it is not the "one" of simple unity, but of compound unity, in the same way as it says of the marriage union, "the twain shall become one flesh";[2] no one would take this to mean that the man and the woman are not two distinct persons.

The Bible commences with the statement, "In the beginning *Elohim* . . ." which is a plural word for God, and prepares us for that mysterious verse in which we find God soliloquizing in the plural, "Let *us* make man in *our* image."[3] Why the "us" and the "our"? How do we reconcile "our image" with the statement of the next verse, "God created man in

---

[1] Deuteronomy 6:4; cp. James 2:19.   [2] Matthew 19:5.
[3] Genesis 1:26.

his own image"? The serpent said of the forbidden tree, "In the day ye eat thereof . . . ye shall be as God, knowing good and evil"; and when they had eaten "Jehovah said, Behold, the man is become as *one of us*, to know good and evil."[1] Such passages are inexplicable according to the unitarian concept that insists on God being a single Person. "God is love" is one of the profoundest statements of the Bible relative to the nature of God, and was true of him before the beginning of time, or the first creature was created. But how can love exist in isolation? Let the reader ponder Augustine's thought-provoking dictum: "If God is love, then there must be in him a Lover, a Beloved, and a Spirit of love."

A Moslem law student who had been given a Gospel of John brought it back with the request that the opening statement might be explained. Said he, "This book speaks of one called the Word of God, and says he was both with God and was God. How can a person be with himself?" The Christian replied, "If there was a problem in mathematics that you could not solve, and you took it to your tutor and he could not solve it, it would at least be clear that neither you nor the tutor had invented the problem. Now here is a problem, not in mathematics but in theology, that is, the being and nature of God as a trinity. Thousands of the ablest minds of the centuries have pondered this problem, and no one has been able to explain it; who then invented it? What man can invent man can explain; what man cannot

―――――――――――――――――――――――
[1] Genesis 3:5,22; cp. 11:7; Isaiah 6:8.

explain man cannot have invented. It must be a revelation." Needless to say, he found no answer to this.

Some pour scorn on the doctrine of the Trinity simply because it is a mystery. This would imply that to them there are no mysteries in the Godhead: all is simplicity. It would appear that they worship a God that they can comprehend within the narrow confines of their finite understanding. "Canst thou find out the Almighty unto perfection? It is high as heaven; what canst thou do? Deeper than Sheol; what canst thou know?"[1] Present to us "a god" whom we can comprehend and explain, who has ceased to be in his infinite being shrouded in mystery, and we will refuse to worship this creation of your finite mind, and from his holy habitation the God of heaven will thunder: "Thou thoughtest that I was altogether such an one as thyself: but I will reprove thee."[2]

CONCLUSION

Before the first coming of Christ, men might hide their real attitude to the Almighty by lightly professing their devotion to an invisible, intangible God. Their conception of God was often vague, shadowy, and unreal. But when in the fullness of time "God sent forth his Son, born of a woman," then the invisible became visible, and the intangible became flesh that men could handle,[3] or mishandle if they chose; God, who is spirit, had become incarnate in the person of his Son, who was "the very image of

---

[1] Job 11:7,8.   [2] Psalm 50:21.   [3] 1 John 1:1.

his substance," the exact representation of God's very being. Now there stood one in the midst of them, whom they knew not, but who was ready to declare, "He that hath seen me hath seen the Father."[1] No longer could men's real heart attitude to their God and Creator be concealed by a vague profession of loving him or believing in him. God had forced man's hand, and thenceforth his attitude to God was to be revealed unmistakably by his attitude to the man Christ Jesus.

This vital truth is emphasized repeatedly in the writings of John the apostle. If you know Christ, you know the Father also;[2] if you believe on Christ, you are in fact believing on the one who sent him;[3] if you confess the Son, you have the Father also.[4] On the other hand, if you honor not the Son, you honor not the Father;[5] if you deny the Son, you have not the Father; if you hate the Son, you hate the Father also.[6] It is therefore a moral and spiritual impossibility to have one attitude to God and quite a different attitude to Christ. You cannot acknowledge the deity of the Father and deny the deity of the Son, for a denial of the Son constitutes a denial of the Father. Whether or not you understand it, whether or not you believe it, your attitude to Christ is your attitude to God. "What think ye of Christ?" is now the acid test of your relationship to God, and your answer will determine the destiny of your soul. Listen to his own solemn words, "Except ye believe that I am, ye shall die in your sins."[7]

---

[1] John 14:9.   [2] John 8:19; 14:7.   [3] John 12:44.
[4] 1 John 2:23.   [5] John 5:23.   [6] John 15:23.
[7] John 8:24 marg.

What think ye of Christ? is the test
To try both your state and your scheme;
You cannot be right in the rest
Unless you think rightly of him.
As Jesus appears to your view,
And he is beloved or not,
So God is disposed to you—
And mercy or wrath is your lot.

Some take him a creature to be—
A man, or an angel at most,
But they have not feelings like me,
Nor know themselves wretched and lost;
So guilty, so helpless am I,
I durst not confide in his blood,
Nor on his protection rely—
Unless I were sure he is God.

John Newton

Any doctrinal scheme which denies the full deity or true humanity of the Son of God, is a faith without foundations, and all its accompanying tenets are suspect.

•   •   •   •

Johann Dannecker (1758-1841), the great sculptor, yearned to give the world a masterpiece that would be treasured forever. He gave himself to prayer and contemplation. One evening as he read his New Testament, he came across these words, "without controversy great is the mystery of godliness."[1] Over-

---

[1] 1 Timothy 3:16.

awed by these lines, he read them again and again. "If only I could catch their spirit and express it in marble," he said to himself. He prayed for grace and guidance. His whole personality and genius were consecrated to the task.

He completed at length the first cast of his statue of the divine Christ. He invited a group of children to visit his studio to inspect his work. They gazed admiringly at the stately figure, and then one boy exclaimed, "He must be a very *great* man!" Dannecker was bitterly disappointed. The impression of greatness was not the one he had wished to convey. He thanked the children and dismissed them. Having set to work and completed his second cast, he sent for a fresh group of children to visit him. Smiling appreciatively, they were magnetically drawn to the lovely figure on the pedestal. It was a girl who broke the silence: "He must have been a very *good* man!" she exclaimed. Dannecker, though encouraged, was by no means satisfied. He decided to make a third attempt. When the final cast had been completed, he sent again for a group of children. Garbed in his long white overalls he scrutinized their faces as they entered the studio. This time, with bated breath, he watched the boys snatch off their caps, while one of the girls fell on her knees. Dannecker felt that at last he had expressed the *adoration* that was in his heart.

In these pages there has been presented to you, not with the art of a sculptor or the brush of an artist, but with the pen of a disciple, a portrait of

Christ. Let the reader bear witness that the lines and features of this portrait do not consist of a few proof texts, or a few isolated passages wrested from their context, but are drawn from the whole manifestation of Jesus Christ as the Bible presents him. "What think ye of Christ?" Pause and view him yet again. He is called the Alpha and the Omega, the First and the Last, the King of kings and Lord of lords, the mighty God, the Father of Eternity, the Lord of Glory, the Prince or Author of life, and Lord of all. See him existing beside the Father before time began, the outshining of his glory, and the very image of his substance, in whom dwells all the fullness of the Godhead bodily. Behold him who is the Creator of the universe, without whom nothing was made that was made; the upholder of all things; the searcher of hearts; the pardoner of sins; the Saviour and Redeemer of men; the bestower of eternal life; the pourer out of the divine Spirit; the quickener of the dead, having the keys of Death and of Hades; and the judge of the universe. Remember that he claims to have exclusive knowledge of the Father, and exclusive power to reveal him to men; to share equally the honor due to the Father, and with the Father to be trusted, implored, and worshipped by creature man. Will you dare to say that he is only a creature, separated from his own Creator by a measureless gulf? Will you merely acknowledge him as a great man? Will you only applaud him as a good man? Or will you adore him as the God-man?

It may be you have recognized who he is for the

first time. Or perhaps it has never occurred to you to doubt that he is the divine Christ. Whichever it be, will you now examine yourself whether you be in the faith? It is possible that your faith in who he is may be no more than a mental assent to a doctrinal fact, rather than a believing in the heart, a faith that saves and transforms, that unites you to the one in whom you believe and so brings you to God. The new sphere of the one who believes is "in Christ"; are you in Christ? "If any man is in Christ, he is a new creature";[1] are you a new creature? "The old things have passed away; behold, they are become new";[1] has that happened in your experience? You cannot afford to be other than crystal clear on this vital issue. Your heart attitude to Christ determines the destiny of your soul.

There stands before you, as there stood long ago in the upper room, the crucified, yet risen Christ. He is no phantom, no illusion, no spirit. He says, "See my hands and my feet, that it is I myself: handle me, and see; for a spirit hath not flesh and bones, as ye behold me having."[2] Yes, he is real, and he comes to us bearing in his resurrection body the proof of his passion. This divine Redeemer was wounded for your transgressions, bruised for your iniquities, the punishment—the price of your peace—was laid upon him, and with his stripes you may be healed.[3] The love that for your sake brought him from the throne of glory to the cross of shame has not diminished with the passing of the centuries. He says, "Come

---

[1] 2 Corinthians 5:17.   [2] Luke 24:39.   [3] Isaiah 53:5.

unto me." Will you fall at his pierced feet in true repentance, in living faith, in glad submission, and say with Thomas, "My Lord and my God"?[1]

---

[1] John 20:28.

APPENDIX

The following is a list of some Old Testament passages referring to Jehovah, which are shown in the New Testament to refer to Christ. They speak for themselves.

Isaiah 40:3,4. "The voice of one that crieth, Prepare ye in the wilderness the way of Jehovah, make straight in the desert a highway for our God."

Matthew 3:1–3. "John the Baptist . . . this is he that was spoken of by Isaiah the prophet, saying, The voice of one crying in the wilderness, Make ye ready the way of the Lord. . . ."

Luke 1:76. "Yea and thou, child [John the Baptist], shalt be called the prophet of the Most High: for thou shalt go before the face of the Lord [Christ] to make ready his ways."

Jeremiah 11:20. "O Jehovah of Hosts . . . that triest the reins and the heart."

Jeremiah 17:10. "I Jehovah search the heart, I try the reins."

Revelation 2:18,23. "These things saith the Son of God . . . I am he which searcheth the reins and hearts."

Isaiah 60:19. "Jehovah shall be unto thee an everlasting light, and thy God thy glory."

Luke 2:30–32. (Simeon speaking of the infant Jesus) "My eyes have seen thy salvation, which thou hast prepared before the face of all peoples; a light for revelation to the Gentiles, and the glory of thy people Israel."

Isaiah 8:13,14. "Jehovah of Hosts . . . He shall be . . . for a stone of stumbling and for a rock of offence."

1 Peter 2:7,8. "But for such as disbelieve . . . [Christ is] a stone of stumbling, and a rock of offence."

Isaiah 45:22,23. "I am God, and there is none else. By myself have I sworn, the word is gone forth from my mouth in righteousness, and shall not return, that unto me every knee shall bow, every tongue shall swear."

Philippians 2:10,11. "That in the name of Jesus every knee should bow . . . and that every tongue should confess that Jesus Christ is Lord, to the glory of God the Father."

Zechariah 12:10. "I [Jehovah] will pour upon the house of David . . . the spirit of grace and of supplication; and they shall look unto me whom they have pierced."

John 19:34–37. "One of the soldiers with a spear pierced his side . . . for these things came to pass that the scripture might be fulfilled . . . They shall look on him whom they pierced."

Malachi 3:1. "Behold, I send my messenger, and

he shall prepare the way before me: and the Lord, whom ye seek, shall suddenly come to his temple."

Matthew 11:10. "This is he [John the Baptist], of whom it is written, Behold, I send my messenger before thy face, who shall prepare thy way before thee."

Genesis 14:19. "God Most High, possessor of heaven and earth."

Deuteronomy 10:14. "Unto Jehovah thy God belongeth the heaven, and the heaven of heavens, the earth, with all that therein is."

John 3:35. "The Father loveth the Son, and hath given all things into his hand."

Acts 10:36. "Jesus Christ (he is Lord of all)."